Ramadan and Id-ul-Fitr

Nancy Dickmann

www.raintreepublishers.co.uk
Visit our website to find out
more information about
Raintree books.

To order:
☎ Phone 0845 6044371
▤ Fax +44 (0) 1865 312263
▨ Email myorders@raintreepublishers.co.uk

Customers from outside the UK please telephone +44 1865 312262

Edited by Sian Smith, Nancy Dickmann, and Rebecca Rissman
Designed by Steve Mead
Picture research by Elizabeth Alexander
Production by Victoria Fitzgerald
Originated by Capstone Global Library Ltd
Printed and bound in China by South China Printing Company Ltd

ISBN 978 0 431 00753 3
14 13 12 11 10
10 9 8 7 6 5 4 3 2 1

British Library Cataloguing in Publication Data
Dickmann, Nancy.
    Ramadan and Id-ul-Fitr. -- (Holidays and festivals)
    1. Ramadan--Pictorial works--Juvenile literature. 2. Id
al-Fitr--Pictorial works--Juvenile literature.
    I. Title II. Series
    394.2'657-dc22

Acknowledgements
We would like to thank the following for permission to reproduce
photographs: Alamy pp. **5** (© Louise Batalla Duran), **8** (© T. Kopecny),
10 (© Art Directors & TRIP), **11**, **23 top** (© imagebroker), **15** (© David
Noble Photography), **19** (© Sally and Richard Greenhill); Corbis pp. **4**, **23
bottom** (© epa), **20** (© Arshad Arbab/epa); Getty Images pp. **13** (Gen
Nishino/Taxi), **14** (Chumsak Kanoknan), **16** (Marco Di Lauro/The Image
Bank), **18** (arabianEye); Photolibrary pp. **7** (Paul Thuysbaert/GraphEast),
21 (Corbis); Shutterstock pp. **6** (© Distinctive Images), **9** (© Dennis Albert
Richardson), **12** (© Kate Fredriksen), **22 left** (© gpalmer), **22 right** (©
Faraways), **23 middle** (© Serp); World Religions Photo Library p. **17**.

Front cover photograph of Muslims celebrating the end of Ramadan,
Colombo, Sri Lanka reproduced with permission of Photolibrary (Dominic
Sansoni/Imagestate RM). Back cover photograph reproduced with
permission of Alamy (© Art Directors & TRIP).

We would like to thank Diana Bentley, Dee Reid, Nancy Harris, and
Richard Aubrey for their invaluable help in the preparation of this book.

Every effort has been made to contact copyright holders of material
reproduced in this book. Any omissions will be rectified in subsequent
printings if notice is given to the publishers.

Contents

What is a festival?

A festival is a time when people come together to celebrate.

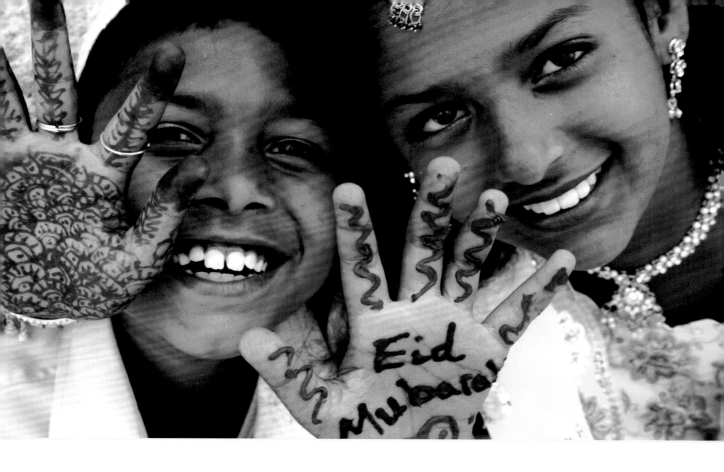

Muslim people celebrate Ramadan and Id-ul-Fitr.

Ramadan

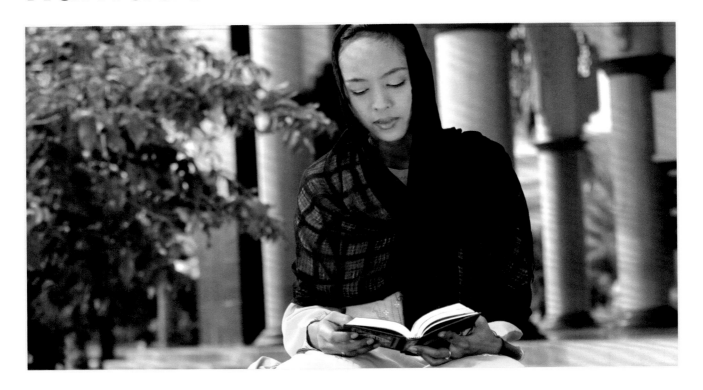

Ramadan is the holiest month for Muslim people.

It is a time to feel close to Allah, or God.

People pray during Ramadan.

mosque

They pray in a mosque.

People may eat before the sun
comes up.

People should not eat or drink during the day. This is called fasting.

People may eat again when the sun goes down.

Ramadan lasts for a month.

Id-ul-Fitr

At the end of Ramadan, Muslim people celebrate Id-ul-Fitr.

new moon

People wait until they see the new moon.

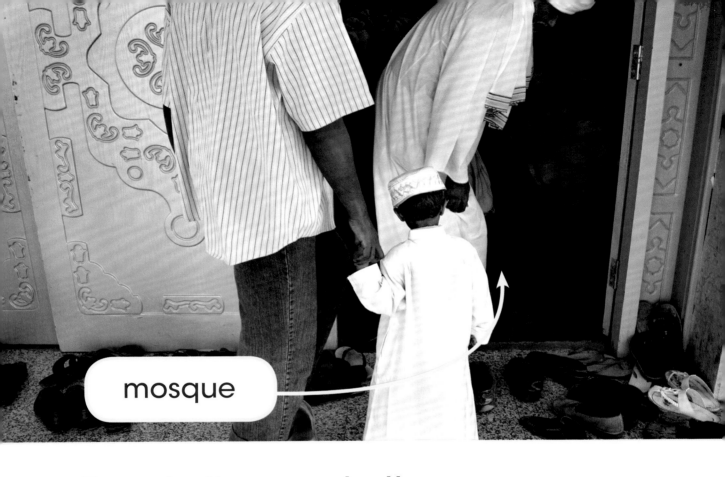

mosque

People then go to the mosque to pray.

People can stop fasting. They can eat at any time.

People visit friends and family.

They share a special meal.

They give food to the poor.

They share sweets and gifts.

Things to look for

new moon

sweets

Have you seen these things?
They make people think of Ramadan
and Id-ul-Fitr.

Picture glossary

 fasting to go without food and water

 mosque building where Muslims go to worship

 Muslim people people who follow the teachings of the religion Islam

Index

Notes for parents and teachers

Before reading

Ask the children to think of as many holidays and festivals as they can. Look at the list together and discuss which holidays and festivals are religious. Explain that Ramadan and Id-ul-Fitr are festivals celebrated by Muslim people, who follow the religion of Islam. Ramadan is a holy time for Muslims because the verses of the Qur'an (the Muslim holy book) were revealed to the prophet Muhammad (pbuh*) during this month. Reading the Qur'an is an important part of Ramadan. The festival of Id-ul-Fitr comes after Ramadan and means the 'festival of breaking of the fast'.

After reading

• Explain that remembering the poor is another important part of Ramadan, and that fasting (explained on page 11) can be a way for people to remind themselves of what it is like to be poor. Ask the children if they can think of ways to help the poor in the local area.

• Ask the children if there are things that they would find it hard to go without. Encourage them to choose something (such as computer games or snacks) to give up for a day or a week. Afterwards, discuss what it was like to go without something they wanted. Explain that during Id-ul-Fitr, Muslims thank Allah for the help and strength that he gave them throughout Ramadan to help them practise self-control.

* Peace be upon him